W9-BFS-687

SAN FRANCISCO

This book was devised and produced by
Multimedia Publications (UK) Ltd

Editor: Marilyn Inglis
Design: John Strange and Associates
Picture Research: Catherine Blackie,
Tessa Paul
Production: Arnon Orbach

Copyright © Multimedia Publications
(UK) Ltd 1984

All rights reserved. No part of this book may
be reproduced or transmitted in any form or
by any means, electronic or mechanical,
including photocopying, recording, or by any
information storage retrieval system, without
permission in writing from the publisher.

ISBN 0 8317 7678 1

First published in the United States of
America 1984 by Gallery Books, an imprint of
W. H. Smith Publishers Inc., 112 Madison
Avenue, New York, NY 10016

Originated by D. S. Colour International Ltd,
London.
Typeset by Flowery Typesetters Ltd.
Printed by Sagdos, Milan, Italy.

SAN FRANCISCO

Carole Chester

GALLERY BOOKS
An Imprint of W. H. Smith Publishers Inc.
112 Madison Avenue
New York City 10016

Contents

The City
By The Bay

It has been saluted in song, romanticized in print, captured forever in countless photographs. At one time, the golden city of San Francisco was where most Americans wanted to live. Yet, it's earthquake prone, often misty and, in some areas, downright seedy. So what accounts for this city's charm?

Like Rome, San Francisco is draped over seven hills. Faded pastel-colored houses, often fatigued-looking and crumbling, cling stubbornly to inclines. At every turn, a vantage point shows some new vista. From Golden Gate Promenade, view the spires of the famous bridge, the golden dome of the Palace of Fine Arts and, beyond, the blue Pacific. From Coit Tower, gaze across the bay to Sausalito and Tiburon. From Cliff House, look down to the offshore Seal Rocks where sea-lions frolic.

It's a city with an outstanding geographic position, but one which took early explorers years to find. They sailed up and down the California coast in search of what was to become San Francisco Bay, but, after Mission Dolores was founded in 1776, the hamlet soon became a city. The fur traders came … the railroad builders came … the gold-seekers, adventurers and pioneers came. Immigrant labor arrived in force — Chinese, Japanese and, later, Greeks, Mexicans, Filipinos and Scandinavians.

This mix has made for tolerance. Where else but here the Haight Ashbury hippy kingdom of the '60s, the gay ghettos, the bawdy entertainment, the outrageous fads and fancies. But where else such elegance — the priceless mansions and Victorian façades; the fashionable women toying with green goddess salads; the superb opera house and intrinsic love of the arts.

The scene at the Wharf is hectic. Human juke boxes, jugglers, a lone violinist. Street stalls displaying artwork and handicrafts. Waterfront seafood vendors. Amusement arcades and gimmicky gifts. Piers that have become shopping complexes. The scene in Chinatown is hectic, too. Shops along Grant Avenue crammed with joss sticks, wind chimes, oriental novelties or Chinese sweetmeats and vegetables. Tea houses and fine restaurants.

The cable cars are not just a tourist attraction — San Franciscans find it a good way to get around too.

But tranquility can be found not far away from such city action. In the picturesque Napa Valley, for instance. This is wine country, land of golden grapes, but when the mist descends, the valley looks like a bowl of Irish coffee – another San Francisco treat! Peaceful Muir Woods boasts giant redwoods, trees which once dominated the West. Then there's Russian River country and the orchard region of the Santa Clara Valley.

Back in town, sin if you like. Broadway is literally a nightclub *strip* and encounters are of the extremely close kind in the 'parlors'. Eat sinfully – good food and restaurants are renowned. Drink and be merry – the forerunner of the martini, the 'Martinez cocktail', was invented here. Be sinfully slothful – in Golden Gate Park's hideaways or in some rotating rooftop lounge.

Of course there are don'ts, but in easy-going San Francisco these are few and far between. Never say 'Frisco'. Pronounce Ghiradelli with a hard 'G'. Watch out for 'Grade' or 'Hill' signs – they're soft words for 'steep'. Nob Hill doesn't have a 'k' and Washington Square doesn't have a 'George'. Above all, don't expect that bridge to really be golden-colored – plans to paint it that way have always been turned down.

Facing page From low rise to high rise, San Francisco is one of America's most popular cities with tourists. Magnificent views of the city are to be had from the many different vantage points.

This page left Among the many other buildings vying for attention, the Trans America Building cannot be overlooked. You may start off by hating it, but come to love its gracefulness. It seems to follow you around wherever you go in the city.

Below One of the most impressive buildings of the Civic Center is the San Francisco City Hall at the end of Fulton Street. It is a superb baroque masterpiece of granite and marble. It was modeled on the Capitol in Washington D.C., but its 300 feet tall gold decorated dome makes it higher than the Washington version.

Facing page There are literally thousands of restaurants in San Francisco, including some very fine Chinese ones. Although not all of the latter are located in Chinatown, Grant Avenue is a good place to start looking.

This page right Cable cars have their own signals! Invented in San Francisco at the turn of the century, cable cars were used to haul passengers up and down hills which were too steep for horse-drawn carriages. They have a very special place in the hearts of the San Franciscans, who have vowed never to let them disappear, but instead maintain them at great financial loss.

Below San Francisco is home to the largest Asian community outside the Orient. In the nineteenth century Chinatown was a ghetto for unwelcome immigrants; now its 24 blocks are proudly nationalistic. Grant Avenue, the main thoroughfare, is lined with hundreds of restaurants and takeaways, souvenir shops and oriental grocery stores.

Facing page Golden Gate Bridge has many moods, but it is always beautiful. Engineer Joseph Strauss gets most of the credit for this fine piece of work, which was completed in 1937. The bridge links San Francisco with Marin County, and its delicacy and apparent fragility make it one of the most beautiful sights in the world.

This page above Coit Tower crowns Telegraph Hill, rising 210 feet from the hill's summit. The tower was built as a monument to volunteer firemen (much needed in San Francisco) and its tip represents a fire-hose nozzle. The money was provided by Lillie Hitchcock Coit who became the city's most ardent volunteer after being rescued from a hotel blaze in 1851 at the age of eight. Views from the tower are spectacular – on a clear day you can see Berkeley and the East Bay Hills.

Left Golden Gate Bridge is actually rust colored. Every time the city fathers suggest painting it gold, they are turned down. Few come and are disappointed. The bridge took four years to build – that's how long it would now take to repaint it.

Previous page San Francisco by night. If you want to feast your eyes, go to Twin Peaks, south of downtown, and look down on the city from every angle.

2
Personalities of Contrast

Easy going, tolerant – these are signs of the Californian temperament. Lovers of the outdoors and sunshine, with gold-streaked hair and a year-round tan. These traits are most evident in San Francisco, which bred flower children and sheltered hippies. San Franciscans think themselves refined, but they can be bawdy. They have a high regard for the arts yet their city has a reputation for porn. Personalities of contrast.

Though the Spanish, Mexicans and Russians all had eyes for San Francisco, it was the hordes of gold seekers who swelled its population. In 1848 it was a boom town but by 1850 it had boomed even more – the population was multiplied by 25 as people set up camp here in the hope of striking it rich. After the golden peak declined, many miners returned home but this was one place they didn't leave as a ghost town. There was still farming, fishing and banking to be done.

But it was thanks to gold that there was a stage coach transportation system – in 1860, San Francisco became the terminus of the Pony Express. It was thanks to gold, too, that the earliest banking system came about – there were already 19 banks in this city in 1855. In spite of such organization, there was unrest. The 1850s brought immigrants, especially Chinese, but not enough women to create settled family units. Crime, vice and corruption were a way of life. To combat it came the Vigilantes – a committee formed in San Francisco, over-reacting in their pursuance of law and order. Yet another contrast!

The fame and fortune of individuals gave the city its early gloss. 'The Comstock Lode' (named for the man who discovered the rich deposits of gold and silver) may have been in Nevada, but it enabled San Franciscans to become wealthy and generous. Sutro became mayor and donated a library; Mackay loaned money for an international cable and telegraph system.

Left The catch comes in fresh every afternoon at Fisherman's Wharf. Take your pick from the open-air market, and while you decide what to have for dinner, have an appetizer from one of the seafood stalls.

It was on the busy Market/Powell corner that Comstock millionaire 'Lucky' Baldwin built a hotel. Market Street itself was part of the city layout designed by Jasper O'Farrell in 1847 – extra wide because he believed it would eventually see a lot of traffic. He was right. In San Francisco, it's often the streets themselves which hold interest – Maiden Lane, for example, so pretty today with its terraced walkways, delightful shops and restaurants was, in the 1800s, the very heart of the Red Light District.

Railroad fortunes gave The Big Four their power. Leland Stanford, Collis Huntington and Mark Hopkins founded the Central Pacific Railroad and were later joined by another merchant, Charles Crocker. In 1869 they turned their sights on the San Francisco Bay area, the central valley, and a coastal route to southern California. Another flood of immigrants – Chinese and Irish – came as workers, and The Big Four invested their money in San Francisco.

Money and power gave the city culture, education, fine hotels; brought writers, poets and other celebrities. Yet it was a natural catastrophe – the 1906 earthquake and fire – that ultimately modernized the place. Fires caused by fallen short-circuited electrical wires raged for days and wiped out Nob Hill and Chinatown. The rebuilding that followed created employment and saw such new developments as the cable car system. It brought a new look and enough panache for the city to host the Panama-Pacific Exposition in 1915. Today's San Franciscans are used to earthquakes – their home sits on the San Andreas Fault, after all – and now construct earthquake-proof buildings.

Facing page above Most cable cars have controls at one end only and so have to be turned around at their destination. The turntable allows one man to turn the six-ton car with relative ease – and in this most modern of cities it's a great draw for the tourists.

Below Another of those streets which makes San Francisco famous. As usual the cable car is heavily loaded. Sometimes this century-old tradition of traveling at nine miles per hour causes problems for other drivers, who are obliged to stop every time a cable car halts in front of them. But good-humored tolerance usually prevails.

This page above The most scenic of the remaining cable car routes is from Powell-Hyde to the northern waterfront. If you develop a passion for cable cars, you could visit the Cable Car Barn to see where the power for all those underground cables comes from, and to delve into the history of the system.

Below Girlie shows and sleazy bars are mostly found along Broadway in San Francisco's North Beach area. It was here that the 'topless' fashion was born in 1964. In between the neon signs inviting you to all kinds of sex shows, there are good nightclubs to be found as well.

People have become legendary in San Francisco and given their names to many a tourist sight. The beloved Mark Twain worked here for a time as a reporter, while the less familiar Lotta Crabtree (taught to sing and dance by the notorious Lola Montez) has a fountain named for her. Scottish landscape gardener John McLaren created much of Golden Gate Park and there's a Rhododendron Dell which bears his name.

People have given the city its unique atmosphere – to the Asians, a reminder of Asia; to the Europeans, a reminder of Europe. Neighborhoods merge with neighborhoods because physically the city is small. The west side, for example, is mainly residential and known as The Avenues – an area of parks and museums. The eight-block Civic Center is the hub of political and cultural life with its fine halls and impressive buildings. Down by the marina are some of the loveliest vistas and around Union Square, some of the best shops. The financiers are on Montgomery Street; the elite cling to the hills.

Chinatown

It's the largest Asian community outside of Asia – a city within a city. Through the green-tiled gate at Bush Street along the main artery, Grant Avenue is – and always has been – a Chinese community, now bursting at its seams in every direction from a growing Chinese American population, plus new Eastern immigrants.

In 1850, Little Chinatown was just that – a small settlement on Upper Sacramento and Dupont Streets. It grew and flourished and with it, opium dens and brothels. Some of the worst were in St. Mary's Square, today a peaceful oasis within the busy hum of Chinese life. Waverly Place was also a notorious alley for prostitution, gambling dens and Tong warfare – today it's one of Chinatown's prettiest streets.

The restaurants, bars and curio shops that line Grant Avenue resemble a mini Hong Kong dedicated to pleasing the tourist, while the cross streets and parallel Stockton Street are more inscrutable, more Asian. Few joss houses survive, but the Kong Chow Temple on Pine Street and the Tin How Temple are two that remain.

Facing page above Chinatown is full of interesting tea houses, back alleys and pagoda-topped buildings. Two places not to miss are the Chinese Cultural Center, which sponsors walking tours of old Chinatown, and the Chinese Historical Society, which shows how the Chinese contributed to the Gold Rush.

Below The ornamental green-tiled gate at Bush Street marks the entrance to Chinatown and gives you a taste of the oriental scene which follows. Dragons and pagodas abound in a color scheme of red, green and gold. While some of this is to attract tourists, much is for the Chinese themselves who live in the cross streets off Grant Avenue, which remain very Asian.

This page above The Japanese community is much smaller than the Chinese, and Japantown does not look very different from the rest of San Francisco. But every year national pride is displayed in the celebrations of the Cherry Blossom Festival.

Center Chinatown attracts many sightseers, but it is also home for many Chinese. A break for these Chinese men means a game or two of checkers or mah-jong.

Below For many years the Chinese kept to their own city within a city. Now the burgeoning population of Chinese Americans and more recent Asian immigrants have burst old boundaries in all directions.

Little Italy

You won't find Little Italy on a map—its real name is North Beach. And if you look for a beach, you won't find one—it disappeared over a century ago when landfill operations began. The Italian quarter, which centers on Broadway and Columbus Avenue, has been severely nudged by Chinatown's expansion but the older generation remains firmly implanted around Telegraph Hill.

The best espressos and bakeries are located here along with serious drinking bars and inexpensive restaurants. Broadway, too, is the nightclub belt where the pitch is topless, bottomless, female wrestlers and live sex acts, competing with quality, better-grade nightlife. Outdoors, spectating can be done in Washington Square where people-watching is the norm. For higher-level indoor viewing, there's the Museo Italo-Americano.

This page left It's a sunny day in San Francisco and time to catch a little sun. One thing's sure, he would have to be much more outrageous to turn any heads in this city.

Below Polk Street, between Geary and Pacific Avenues, is where many of the city's substantial gay population live. San Francisco has always been proud of its tolerant attitudes: In 1977 its "Gay Freedom Day" march attracted about 200000 people. However, it's called by some the "gay ghetto of the world".

Facing page right A touch of the Hari Krishnas. Wandering minstrels such as these, of all and any nationality, are often to be seen throughout the city.

Below Is it Halloween? Or are they street artists preparing for a performance? It could be either, but in San Francisco any time's a good time for dressing up and cavorting.

The Latin District

People of various Latin nationalities share San Francisco space, many living around Mission Dolores. Mexican Americans comprise the largest group – not surprisingly since the Mexicans were among the first to arrive in California and later returned as immigrants hunting work. But now they've been joined by El Savadoreans, Chileans and other Latins, creating their own ghetto. The district sprawls in all directions from 24th Street and Mission Street, its central core. Art galleries and arts and crafts shops featuring Central and South American goods predominate on Mission Street along with a galaxy of inexpensive restaurants.

Gay San Francisco

Perhaps it's the arts, perhaps the city's jewel-like setting or simply the live-and-let-live attitude that has attracted so large a number of homosexuals that they've established their own community. Most of the gay population live near commercial Polk Street, between Geary Street and Pacific Avenue, or Castro Street, south of Market Street to 19th Street.

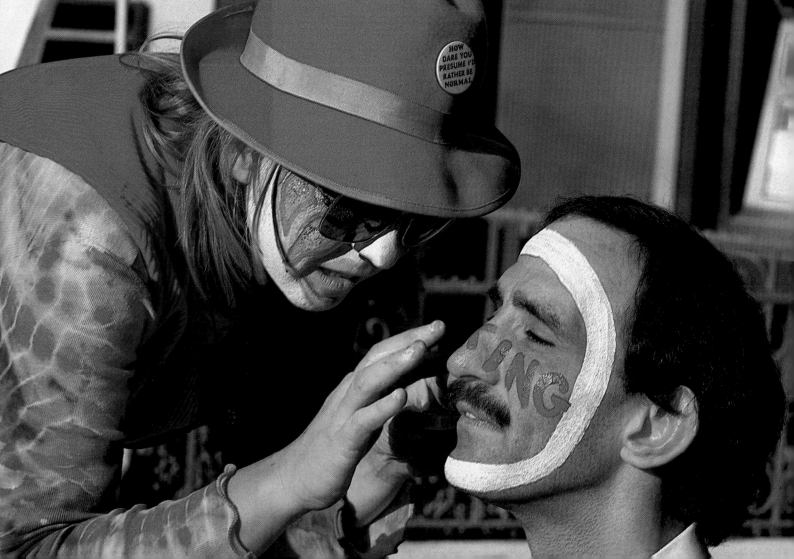

Hippie San Francisco

Being – or not being – a hippie depends on the interpretation. Is it different dress, a particular way of thinking, a philosophical outlook, or simply drugs? Back in the '60s some weren't sure and Haight Ashbury got itself a bad name. Drug abuse and riots put this particular North Beach section on the whole of America's map. The area has ceased to be strife-torn, though it remains seedy and unkempt. Some eccentrically-dressed folk and some downright eccentrics lurk aimlessly, but apart from them there's really not a lot to see. Most artisans and dropouts have moved north to Mendocino – low-key, pretty, and just that bit too far away for a one-day excursion.

Student San Francisco

Everyone has heard of Berkeley. A visit to this university is a good excuse to cross the Oakland Bay Bridge and enjoy the views of the city, bay and other bridges, particularly impressive from the marina. The campus itself is sprawling and prestigious, though its students are likely to reflect the mood of the day. A self-guided tour will show you the Lawrence Hall of Science, the Art Museum, Loewy Museum of Anthropology and the Botanical Gardens.

Young San Francisco

Is San Francisco a city for children? It's not number one on the California list but there are things to see and places to go that will interest kids. The city's own zoo, where gorillas are the prime attraction, is one choice, the Steinhart Aquarium another.

Science lessons in the form of games – fun and a painless way for children to learn – can be found at the Exploratorium in the Palace of Fine Arts and in Berkeley's Lawrence Hall of Science. Most of the theme parks are located closer to Los Angeles, but Marriotts Great America in the Santa Clara Valley is within reach. Cartoon characters, thrill rides, craft demonstrations and all-day cinema and theater ensure the stiff entrance price gives value for money.

Facing page Exotic restaurants abound; this one, Maxwell's Plum, glitters.

Left The city center has many streets named for early pioneers like Geary and Kearny. Go downtown for your shopping or to find a hotel.

Below A fisheye view of the city taken as this workman repairs the Golden Gate Bridge.

Facing page above A suburb with a difference
– Richmond.

Below Waves crash onto the beach at Lookout
Point.

This page left An artist on the San Francisco
waterfront sketches the Golden Hind II.

Below Joggers are everywhere.

From Victoriana to High Tech

In a certain light, when sunshine filters through, it may look gold, but in reality the Golden Gate Bridge is rust-colored. No matter. It's the symbol of this great city, the best place for viewing the San Francisco skyline, and for many years was the world's longest suspension bridge. It's a true feat of engineering and visually pleasing to the eye.

It is indeed its visual pleasures that make San Francisco such a heart-stealer. Kipling may have termed it a 'mad city', but then it is. There is no uniformity to its architecture or attitudes. Baroque domed palaces mix with tired Victorian houses; impressive spires and towers rise in a mixture of shapes and sizes.

The Golden Gate is not the only bridge to span the bay. There's San Francisco-Oakland Bay Bridge – in a suspension span between the city and Yerba Buena Island and in cantilever form on to Oakland – and the Richmond-San Raphael Bridge connects the Marin and Contra Costa shores.

If there's any one landmark building, it's the Trans America, said to be the first earthquake-proof structure, a pyramid of an office block. San Francisco's oddities have become tourist attractions. A crooked street that hairpin bends eight times in a single block – Lombard – is a triumph if maneuvered by car. Cable cars, invented to carry passengers up and down hills too steep for horse-drawn carriages, but kept simply because they're loved. Only three of the lines still exist: Powell-Mason and Powell-Hyde from Powell Street to the waterfront, and the line from Market Street to Van Ness Avenue.

Left One of the delights of the San Franciscan peninsula is Stanford University, seen here from the Hoover Tower. The campus spreads for thousands of acres around Palo Alto, and one of its most striking attractions is the Venetian mosaic of the Sermon on the Mount which can be seen on the facade of the Memorial Church.

This page right Frank Lloyd Wright designed this building.

Below One of Frank Lloyd Wright's last great public buildings is the Marin County Civic Center. The interior has a towering central court with hanging gardens. The building houses government offices and so cannot be toured, but visitors are welcome to stroll in the surrounding gardens.

Unique and ugly is the monument at the junction of Market and Geary Streets – Lotta's Fountain. It was named for Lotta Crabtree. Lotta toured the mining camps to much applause, and the fountain in her name was given to the city in 1875. The three-tiered, pagoda-style building in Chinatown now houses the Bank of Canton but used to be the Chinese Telephone Exchange. Chinatown has its own wax museum, historical society and several churches of which the most interesting is Old St. Mary's, built in 1854 with granite brought from China.

From its early days, San Francisco has had strong connections with banking. A founder of the Bank of California built the Mills Building but The Pacific Coast Stock Exchange is more impressive. The Bank of America takes up a whole block.

The most celebrated name, Wells Fargo, is a bank with a history room that shows brigands' mementoes and features a genuine Wells Fargo coach. Nineteenth-century bankers and politicians gathered at the saloon which once stood on the corner of Montgomery and Washington.

Money … gold … this city was full of it. At the Bank of California today you can see how gold looked to the miners who found it. At the old San Francisco Mint, gold to the tune of $10 million is on display together with privately minted coins.

Left San Francisco's 40 hills make it one of the most easily recognizable cities of the world.

Right San Franciscans are proud of both old and new, and the city boasts many lovingly preserved Victorian homes. Here the old and new stand side by side.

The Hills

Money went to the hills to build mansions and money remains there today. Nob Hill especially, a hill of palaces so ornate that citizens of an earlier era rode up there by cable car simply to gape. Those palaces were the homes of railroad tycoons and silver kings. The Stanford Court Hotel stands on the site of the first Big Four mansion – that belonging to Leland Stanford. The Mark Hopkins Hotel is on the spot where the railroad millionaire built his place; the Fairmont Hotel on the site chosen by silver king James Fair.

Much of Nob Hill was demolished by the 1906 fire but silver king James Flood's place survived. It was the first brownstone to be built out West and cost $1½ million at the time. These days it is the very exclusive Pacific Union Club. Charles Crocker built his mansion on top of Nob Hill, a commanding site now taken up by Grace Cathedral. Its construction began in 1910 but the cathedral contains far older treasures: an 11th-century French altar; some 16th-century Flemish carvings and an English 44-bell carillon.

Russian Hill is far less formal and preferred by writers and artists. The first home on this hill was built in 1852 but an apartment block now occupies its site. There is little reminder of the 1800s save two octagonal houses: a private Green Street home and another on Gough Street, open to the public. The design was popular in the 1850s as a means of catching the sunlight. Recommended starting place for a tour of the Russian Hill district is the Haas-Lilienthal House, a Victorian masterpiece.

Few people thought of living on Telegraph Hill in the early days but later it became base for the Italian community. Surgeon's daughter Lillie Coit paid for Coit Tower, a memorial to volunteer firemen, to be built here in 1934. It's an unimpressive structure in itself but provides a marvelous view on a clear day when you can see to the far shore, Berkeley, the mission district and beyond.

All of the Telegraph Hill area survived the big fire. Both the Californian Steam and Navigation Building (1859) and the Ship Building still stand. Several flatiron buildings – such as Columbus Tower – can be seen on Columbus Avenue, but the worst of the nearby Barbary Coast (home of brothels and dives) was destroyed and now there are more interior decorators than there are B girls.

The Waterfront

Once there was plenty of space to make boat repairs at the wharves by the foot of Taylor Street. Then came the first restaurant catering for fishermen; many more followed. Fisherman's Wharf today could be renamed Tourist's Wharf – crowded and curious. The Maritime Museum, though, explains much of the city's maritime past in an enjoyable way. An old car ferry, steam schooner, scow and side-wheel tugboat,

Facing page below The mission system was established by the Spanish to convert the Indians and to gain Spanish allegiance. Some missions like that of San Francisco grew into a city, but kept the Spanish name.

This page above This is Mission Dolores and the pretty rooftops and tower of the basilica. Its white walls are four feet thick and the few windows glazed to keep out the hot sun. The Mission is an historical landmark, but remains a living church as well.

Below The basilica of Mission Dolores now dwarfs the adjoining mission chapel.

Right History lies buried in the old graveyard adjoining the mission chapel. The names inscribed on headstones here are those of early pioneers.

berthed at Hyde Street Pier, may all be inspected, while the museum building itself houses models, photographs and a mass of memorabilia. Between pier and museum stretches Aquatic Park. Wine history comes up at the Wine Museum, all the way from vine to vino and glass.

As for a Wharf landmark, the choice would be between Ghiradelli Square and The Cannery. The former was originally a chocolate factory which was converted into a fashionable shopping complex. The latter was a fruit and vegetable canning plant until White Russian immigrant Leonard Martin purchased it in 1963 and it, too, became a chic complex of galleries and boutiques. For all that, the Ferry Building has been an Embarcadero feature since 1903 and is still a working terminal.

This page above There are still many beautiful old Victorian houses left in San Francisco. Fillmore Street has some of the best. These days, young families are moving in and renovating them.

Facing page The city's pride in preserving the old, as well as promoting the new, is seen here in McAllister Street's superb examples of wooden Victorian houses.

Below Spiral staircase detail from the Embarcadero.

34

The *Balclutha* can't be missed either. Berthed alongside Pier 43, it's one of the last remaining square riggers from the end of the sail era. Before coming to rest as a historic exhibit, the *Balclutha* had an exciting life – a maiden round-the-Horn voyage in 1887; work in the grain trade; moving lumber to Australia; salmon hauling in Alaska; and even being a showboat.

Unique

The Palace of Fine Arts was meant to be temporary – for the 1915 Panama-Pacific International Exposition – so it was constructed of simple plaster on a light frame. But there was something about its graceful columns and dome overlooking a reflecting pool that made San Francisco want to keep it forever, so it has since been rebuilt in concrete.

Napoleon's 18th-century Parisian palace was magnificently copied for the Californian Palace of the Legion of Honor in Lincoln Park. Not surprisingly, it contains French cultural exhibits and works of art, including a collection of Rodins.

The Presidio was created in the days of the first mission. It's Army headquarters now just as it was then – the Army Museum being San Francisco's oldest adobe building. In the 1880s this military attachment was surrounded by bare sand hills and rocks; in the 1980s, there are trees – 80 000 of them planted during the last 100 years.

Mission Dolores was founded in 1776 by Father Junipero Serra, but not on its present site. The building you see today was built in adobe style in 1782. The old chapel is little changed and many a pioneer lies buried in its graveyard.

This page above Sadly, many wooden Victorian houses were destroyed in the fires following the earthquake of 1906. Those that remain have been taken good care of.

Below Telegraph Hill is one of the city's "golden hills". The Spaniards called it Loma Alta or High Hill, and later it became an Italian district. Buildings here were not destroyed in the great 1906 fire because, so it's said, they were doused with buckets of red Italian wine.

Facing page above San Francisco is a city of contrasts! Here the lights of downtown twinkle in the background, while a quieter rhythm settles on this delightful Victorian residential area.

Below San Francisco is proud of its architectural mix – this 1930s Indian-style house on the corner of Webster and Filbert Street is as much San Francisco as the skyscrapers of downtown.

A mission was a civic center in its time but San Francisco's City Hall certainly looks very different with its golden domes and imposing size. It is part of the Civic Center, a particularly grand cluster of buildings. Work began immediately after the 1906 fire and along with City Hall, the Center comprises the War Memorial Opera House, Veterans Memorial Building, the Civic Auditorium, Main Library and State Building.

It is not only old warehouses that have been put to good use. At Fort Winfield Scott, beneath the San Francisco end of the Golden Gate Bridge, National Park Service personnel dressed in uniforms of the 1860s give troop drills and show off artillery skills.

If passing mention has been made of one or two San Francisco hotels, it's for landmark reasons. Any film with a Pacific setting seems to have an opening or concluding shot from Top of the Mark at the Mark Hopkins. The bar has a 50-mile panoramic view, which possibly explains it! As mentioned before, the hotel is not the house that Mark Hopkins had built – that burned down in 1906 – though it is on the same site. Actually, Hopkins never did live in his mansion here – he died before it was completed.

As truth would have it, James Fair didn't see his property completed either, but it was his daughter who decided to turn the residence into a hotel. Everything went in 1906 except for the granite walls, but it was rebuilt in time for a 1907 opening. The hotel's tower was added much later, as were the exterior glass elevators, but its fashionable customers and service would surely meet with Mr. Fair's approval.

The Sheraton Palace replaced The Palace Hotel which also fell in the blaze of 1906. The original, which opened in 1875, was said to be America's first truly luxurious hotel in the days when class was just money. It had 800 rooms then, was seven storeys high and built on over two acres of ground. A paved marble floor, a glass-domed rotunda, and as much ostentation as could be displayed in one establishment brought a cascade of celebrity guests. This, too, was the place where Hawaii's King Kalkaua died, and where the legendary Diamond Jim Brady ate six dozen oysters in one go. The present day hostelry is far smaller and not so plush, but its past is unlikely to be forgotten.

Right Seen from above, all 853 feet of the Trans American Pyramid can be fully appreciated. It's not just another example of San Franciscan excess – it's designed to be earthquake proof. For a city that sits on a major fault line, that's an important consideration.

Left above Coit Tower.

Below In 1776 the Franciscan Friars established their mission, to convert the local Indians to Christianity, a mile or two south of the Presidio. The mission, officially called San Francisco de Asis, became known as Mission Dolores after a local lake when founding father, Father Palou, said Mass in 1776.

Above The reception area for visitors, not prisoners, on Alcatraz island. The main block with its steel bars, dark cells and mess hall are what most visitors go to see. If you are brave enough you can go into the dark, unlit "Hole" kept for solitary confinement of exceptionally difficult prisoners.

Right Enough to send shivers up your spine — the inside of Alcatraz, the prison from which no one ever escaped alive. The prohibitive running costs led to it being closed down in 1963, but since 1973 it has been open to the public. Ferries leave daily from Pier 43 at Fisherman's Wharf, but now it's a popular trip, so book your place.

Above In 1969 American Indians took over Alcatraz island in protest at the US government treatment of 'native Americans'. Here are some Indian children seen playing with an old truck.

Left Fort Point can be found directly under the San Francisco end of the Golden Gate Bridge. National Park Service personnel dressed in period uniform give troop drills and artillery practice here.

DEPARTMENT OF JUSTICE
BUREAU OF PRISONS

U. S.
GOVERNMENT
FOR OFFICIAL USE
ONLY

The Bounty
of Sun and Sea

Railway barons, bankers and merchants gave San Francisco its notion for fine food and ritzy hotels. They demanded it, they could afford it, and by the 19th century the city had earned itself a justifiable reputation for excellent cuisine. By way of contrast, the railroad workers, the immigrants and the poor needed sustenance of the basic-but-good variety. They spent their money on food, not decor. A restaurant could be plain so long as what its kitchen produced was good. And the immigrants called for a touch of home – something Slavic, something French, certainly something Mexican and Chinese. The end result is food to satisfy every conceivable palate.

Few can resist the Oriental choice – flamed quail, Szechuan spiced beef, minced squib, sushi and sashimi – to be found in Chinatown, Japantown, and beyond. Victor Bergeron's original Trader Vic's is here, offering with great flair the best of Polynesian food and drink. Fans of Italian cooking claim that the pasta served in North Beach restaurants is the best outside of the old country. And no one can deny that Latin and Mexican influences have produced fine and interesting dishes.

If there is typically local food, it is fish – grilled with respect, eaten with awe. Locally caught shrimp, Dungeness crabs and clams are sold in abundance at Fisherman's Wharf. Fresh and fried; eaten from cartons; displayed on marble slabs; bought ready to eat or ready to cook. Red snapper, delicately baked in foil; California sole soothed in a cream sauce; bass smothered in sorrel butter; shark cut thick as steak. All kinds of seafood go into cioppino, a fish stew with peasant origins.

In the frill-free establishments, the old traditional San Francisco eating places with bare wood floors, unadorned walls and bentwood chairs, fish may be cooked before diners' eyes. Only the waiters have changed – younger, very pleasant. Or, beneath gleaming crystal chandeliers amid the plush of turn-of-the-century saloons, steak is served in hefty portions. In the days of gold and garters and massive rancheros,

Left Eating out in San Francisco is a treat – the number and variety of restaurants is almost unlimited.

Facing page With all its other attractions it would be easy to regard the boats as just part of the pretty background picture.

it was beef that kept the blood red, gave speed to the trigger finger. This 'Old San Francisco Steak House' theme now has worldwide appeal.

Any dining spot worth its salt offers a basket of sourdough bread, an unleavened variety unique to San Francisco. But Californians have as sweet a tooth as other Americans so breads are made with fruit and nuts, and cakes and pies with creamy fillings. Fruit comes with everything, as garnish or in sauce. California eats what California grows – dates, oranges, peaches, melons. Avocados and artichokes are staples; walnuts and cherries, bargains.

Salads are of the gourmet, not the wilted, variety. Tender pink prawns heaped high on crisp greens, doused in green goddess dressing – a San Francisco invention. Waldorf salads with nuts; Caesar salads with croutons; spinach salads with bacon.

The majority of the city's famous restaurants are in the section of town bounded by Market Street to the south, Van Ness Avenue to the west and the bay on other sides but there's many an intriguing eating place tucked away in a side street or across the bridges. Fast food outlets are as prevalent as they are elsewhere but one type that San Franciscans especially love is the ice cream parlor.

This page above The Palace of Fine Arts was originally built as a temporary structure for the Panama-Pacific Exposition of 1915. The locals so loved its neo-classical columns and dome that it was rebuilt in concrete. It is the home of the Exploratorium, where science is explained by way of ingenious gadgets.

Below The Palace of Fine Arts from another angle.

According to the cognoscenti, it was a San Francisco barman by the name of Martinez who concocted the forerunner of America's favorite drink – the martini. Whatever the case, it is wine that should be called the speciality of this city. The best vines grow in the valleys north and south of San Francisco, like the most famous of all, Napa. Most growers welcome visitors warmly to tour and sample, learn and buy. It was the Spanish who first brought grape cuttings to California for mission plantings, but it wasn't until the 19th century that wine was produced in earnest by Hungarian, French and German immigrants. Since many of the valleys are only a couple of hours' drive from the city, wine tours are as San Franciscan as sourdough. Camera enthusiasts may prefer April and May or September to November, perhaps opting for a harvest-time visit during this latter period.

Over 100 wineries have established themselves in Napa Valley: small ones which require an appointment to visit; large ones whose wines are widely known; wineries with modern cellars and others with old romantic ones. The valley is only 25 miles long, but dramatic climatic changes allow for a full variety of grapes to flourish: Chardonnay and Cabernet, Pinot Noir and Zinfandel. The cellars at Christian Brothers Greystone Winery are memorable. Robert Mondavi hides up-to-the-minute equipment behind a Spanish colonial façade. Beringer's network of tunnels is interesting and Sterling Vineyards may only be reached by aerial tram.

More grapes grow in rival Sonoma County, a spread of land both historic and picturesque. Though fewer of the wineries here are household names, Sonoma is generally considered the birthplace of wine-making in the area, for a Hungarian named Haraszthy first introduced Zinfandel grapes at his Buena Vista vineyard in the 1850s. Sonoma Valley itself can only boast some 20 cellars but the county houses around 100.

Left The late sixties and early seventies saw a new development phase in San Francisco, but without the claustrophobic effect achieved in New York. The sky was never quite blotted out, and growth has slowed down since then. Here are some of San Francisco's most impressive blocks seen from Ferry Park.

This page The Galleria Shopping Center.

Below You can buy all sorts of shellfish at Fisherman's Wharf – you may find a bargain. But, whatever you find, it will certainly be fresh. If you can't face the thought of cooking, buy something ready-cooked and eat it from a carton, or just sit back and be waited on in any of the numerous restaurants.

47

Mendocino County has a lilting name and two small wine districts – good sources for Chenin Blanc and Johannisberg Riesling, while Livermore Valley in Alameda County was growing Sauvignon Blanc and Sémillon way back in 1880.

The city's diverse entertainment scene can be as brash and vulgar as it was when Chinatown's dens of vice were full to overflowing; as subtle and restrained as your most conservative elderly relative; as fun and vivacious as the liveliest can handle.

Yet, the arts flourished in the 19th century – indeed, 'culture' was at the height of fashion in 1870. By 1879 demand called for year-round opera at the Tivoli Theater and Opera House and, by the end of that century, San Francisco's opera season was America's finest. Music was so loved that it was this city's symphony orchestra which was the first to receive regular help from public funding.

The Opera House and Davies Symphony Hall are both part of the Civic Center but many fine recitals are held at the California Palace of the Legion of Honor in Lincoln Park, while the Music Concourse in Golden Gate Park has an auditorium which holds thousands and presents Sunday band concerts when the weather's good. Though the city is more musically inclined than anything else, it doesn't lack good theaters.

Facing page above Golden Gate Park offers a luscious retreat to city dwellers and sightseers. Development of its thousand acres began in 1868, against all the natural odds, on a site of bare sand dunes. Today the park contains three major museums, as well as beautiful gardens stocked with plants from around the world. These are the M. H. de Young Memorial Museum, one of the largest in the West, the Asian Art Museum and the California Academy of Sciences.

Below The focal point of downtown, Union Square is the heart of the shopping district. The two-and-a-half acre block was presented to the city by John Geary when he was mayor. It is now an ideal resting or meeting place, and every July 4 a cable car bell-ringing contest takes place here.

This page above Charles Crocker, one of the nineteenth-century railroad barons, provided the money to build this Victorian conservatory modeled on Kew Gardens, England. Tropical plants from around the world are permanently on display here, and seasonal flowers can be seen in the exhibition room of the west wing.

Left Within Golden Gate Park is a five acre Japanese Tea Garden. This oriental gem has miniature trees, Shinto shrines and a wishing-well bridge. Is is perhaps at its best in the spring when the cherry blossoms are in full bloom. When you have wandered among the tranquil pools and exotic pagodas, take some jasmine tea in the tea house.

Broadway productions are presented at the Golden Gate Theater and traveling Broadway shows may often be seen at the Curran Theater.

Along Broadway and Columbus Avenue, barkers try to entice customers into sleazy strip bars and other tacky joints. In the Venetian Room at the Fairmont, silver-tongued greats croon and big bands play between shows. Top live entertainment sticks closely to the top hotels, which are also the places to go for a romantic smoochy dance or elegant disco. One Broadway nightspot which has become a phenomenon – it's the city's longest-running attraction – is Finocchio's, where female impersonators do their thing in a savory way.

Comedy, folk music and jazz used to be major league here until the topless rock era took over, but gradually they are regaining popularity. A number of good clubs are in North Beach, others are on the waterfront. Some feature the established, others present promising newcomers.

Down at the Wharf, street entertainers work like mad to earn a buck. A human juke box pops up to mime the latest hit when coins jingle into the slot. A pickup truck moves slowly to give passersby the chance to enjoy the juggler standing on top. A guitarist twangs out a folk song with a refrain catchy enough for others to join in.

Hollywood may make the movies, but San Francisco likes to watch them – porno and the better kind. There are maybe 50 regular movie theaters, many of which show first-run films, but most of them are in residential neighborhoods. You'll find them on Geary Boulevard and Clement Street, on Union Street and Fillmore Street; near Pacific Heights and on Van Ness Avenue to the north of the Civic Center. Downtown can claim only one. The city has its own international film festival held in the fall at the Palace of Fine Arts.

The melee of nationalities has encouraged festivals with fervor. Chinatown is at its most vivacious for Chinese New Year and Cherry Blossom Festival at the Japan Center is rewarding. What is typically American, typically Western, however, is the annual Grand National Rodeo and Horse Show held at the Cow Palace. An appropriately named venue for this event though the Cow Palace equally hosts conventions, rock concerts and other sport tournaments.

Right While you are down at Fisherman's Wharf take time to go along to Pier 39, to the shops and the restaurants on this waterfront conversion.

This page left Avalon Bay Pleasure Pier and Casino.

Below Buskers performing in Golden Gate Park.

5
Westcoast Playground

San Franciscans jog everywhere – in the parks and on the beaches, along specially designed tracks and in residential neighborhoods. It's a civic pastime if not exactly a sport. In Golden Gate Park, countless paths allow jogging enthusiasts to give free reign to mortal energies. Roller skaters show off almost professional talents and cyclists enjoy their freedom in traffic-free space.

The 40-block-long park is a favorite recreational area but it also contains San Francisco's greatest art museum, the M.H. de Young, and an outstanding natural history museum, the California Academy of Sciences. These are in the most developed part of the park, between Stanyan Street and Tenth Avenue. To the north of main John F. Kennedy Drive, the Conservatory of Flowers, modeled after England's Kew Gardens, displays permanently and seasonally, tropical plants and flowers from around the world. South of the drive, in John McLaren Rhododendron Dell, 20 acres of rhododendrons bloom; next to the de Young Museum, a five-acre Japanese Tea Garden is at its most magnificent in March when blanketed in cherry blossoms.

West of the California Academy of Sciences, in Shakespeare's Garden, are examples of every tree, plant and flower the playwright ever mentioned. True botanists head to the Strybing Arboretum and Botanical Gardens where native Californian, foreign and rare plants number in their thousands. Four hundred species of conifer grow in one section alone, and in the Garden of Fragrance flowers pleasant to touch and smell are grown, labeled in Braille for the blind.

Left The Embarcadero is an eight acre area stretching from Fisherman's Wharf to the Ferry building. You can take a tour of the Bay from here, or just browse around the craft stalls or the sculptures.

Stow Lake brings out the boaters—
rowers and canoeists—circling Strawberry
Island. At the Tennis Center, balls are lobbed
and volleyed on 18 hard courts. In the
western part of the park, which is more
open, a par three golf course, a polo field,
equestrian field and fly-casting pools offer
sporting alternatives. For those seeking a
bit of contrast, a small buffalo paddock and
a 47-ton sloop, Amundsen's ship, *Gjoa* are
here as well.

Much of the city's waterfront and all its
ocean beaches come under the heading
Golden Gate National Recreation Area.
Surfers brave the waves at the northern
end of Ocean Beach and hang-gliders take
advantage of the breezes from the bluffs
south of the zoo. Surf fishermen cast their
lines at Baker Beach and picnickers can use
the sheltered sandy beach of Aquatic Park.
Strollers, not swimmers, use the beaches—
waters are chilly, with dangerous currents.

On Municipal Pier, the fishermen wait
and watch for bait to be taken. From the
Wharf, party boats leave for deeper waters.
Yachtsmen anchor in Sausalito's small
harbor and explore the community's stylish
Village Fair shops, or move on to Tiburon
where they patronize the terraced bars and
restaurants that line the waterfront.
Sausalito's Mediterranean-style houses
seem to tumble from steep hills to
shoreline and the view back across the
Golden Gate Bridge to the city is one of the
best. Wealthy Tiburon and Belvedere
homes, too, look snobbishly down from
steep-sided peninsula perches.

Facing page Located in Little Italy, in the North
Beach area of town, Broadway offers a giddy
variety of entertainment.

This page above An evening view of the San
Francisco peninsula seen from Skyline
Boulevard. This lightly-populated slope faces
the Pacific and is often enveloped in mists and
fog. The other side of the peninsula is more
heavily populated with towns cheek by jowl
looking out into the Bay.

Center Ocean Beach, San Francisco's main
beach stretches from the west end of Geary
Boulevard to the city limits. The waves are
good for surfing, but it is dangerous for
swimming and is mainly used by joggers and
walkers.

Below An aerial point of view of the densely
populated suburbs of San Francisco. Houses
set out in this flat grid system are a far cry from
the Victorian mansions covering the famous
hills.

Above San Francisco earned itself a reputation for good food and hotels in the nineteenth century which has only got better. However esoteric your tastes, you will find somewhere in San Francisco to cater for you. Start downtown, and then go where the fancy takes you.

Right The sixties are long since gone, but they are still making music everywhere in San Francisco. From the buskers of Fisherman's Wharf to the more formal summer bands, every taste is catered for.

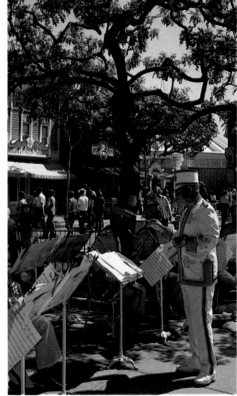

Recreation need only be a leisurely drive along the 49-Mile Scenic Drive marked by signs bearing a white seagull head on a blue background. Motorists can travel west through the Marina District, past the Presidio to Cliff House and Seal Rocks. Offshore, sea-lions frisk on the rocks for most of the year, departing during June or July to breed on Ano Nuevo Island, then returning again to take up landmark residence. Further uphill, at Sutro Heights, lies Adolph Sutro's park.

The Drive leads to Twin Peaks, each nearly 1000 feet high. The Indians and, later, the Spanish, created legendary stories about them, and today they give an excellent vantage point. Five miles south is San Francisco's tallest hill, Mount Davidson, which can be explored only on foot.

For swimmers, there's Fleishhacker Pool or the noisy Playland at Ocean Beach. There's also a boat trip round the harbor or a ferry to Alcatraz from Pier 43. Only a mile offshore, Alcatraz was, until 1963, one of America's most notorious prisons. Before it became a federal penitentiary it served as a fortification, a U.S. military prison and an

Above This giant camera is one of the oddities you can expect to find in a town as crazy and faddish as San Francisco.

Left This 'human jukebox' is just one of the many amateur entertainers to be found at Fisherman's Wharf. Give him a little money and he will strike up his 'orchestra' to play you a unique arrangement. Jugglers, acrobats and other musicians make this one of San Francisco's liveliest spots.

This page right We said that you would find do-it-yourself musicians everywhere in San Francisco. Ghirardelli Square is one of the places where buskers and street theater have been enjoying a world-wide revival.

Below Far from the madding city crowds San Franciscans soak up the sun in Buena Vista Park and, and as the park says, enjoy the beautiful view.

Facing page 'The crookedest street in the world' is Lombard Street, between Hyde Street and Leavenworth Street. The eight switchback bends are a challenge to drivers from all over the world, and the climax of the crazy dipping and climbing of of the San Franciscan hills. Happily, traffic is one-way only.

Army disciplinary barracks. It was opened to the public in 1973, and can provide a shivery experience: for just a second visitors are enclosed in a darkened cell to get a brief taste of the claustrophobia of prison life.

Angel Island, now a state park, is the largest in the bay. In its time it's been a duelling place, a staging area for American soldiers, and a quarantine station. Yerba Buena Island is mostly used by the Navy, and Treasure Island, connected to it, was specially created for the 1939 Golden Gate International Exposition.

Since San Francisco's surrounds are so much a part of it, everyone takes excursions. Not only to the communities just across the bay, but further afield to Napa Valley or Russian River country. There are several missions in the city's vicinity including Santa Clara and San Jose. To reach them, travel through the orchard region of the Santa Clara Valley where some of the fruit Californians love so much is canned and processed. And only 20 miles from the Golden Gate Bridge stands Petaluma, General Vallejo's massive ranch house, today a state historic monument.

Most spectator sports are staged outside of town, though the San Francisco Giants play at Candlestick Park, the Oakland Athletics at the Coliseum.

Shopping

In San Francisco this can be fun. There's a wide choice of goods on offer and the city's compact size makes shopping easy on the feet. Luxury shops and department stores are most numerous on and around Union Square, where benches offer a breather between browsing. This particular block was presented to the city by John Geary – the last mayor under the Spanish system. Major stores include a branch of New York's famous Macy's and Dallas' Neiman-Marcus; other notable names include Saks Fifth Avenue, I. Magnin, Tiffany's and Alfred Dunhill.

All kinds of shops are under one roof at Embarcadero Center in the financial district. You'll find several floors of them in the numbered buildings between Sacramento Street and Clay and Battery and Drumm Streets.

Few shoppers can resist Fisherman's Wharf, where The Cannery and Ghiradelli Square are among the first examples of building conversions into elite shopping complexes, and Pier 39 one of the newer ones. The waterfront is equally a place for picking up a trinket or two or having a portrait painted on the spot. For seekers of souvenirs and curios, Chinatown is the place to go.

The antique quarter tends to be along Union Street, between Van Ness Avenue and Fillmore Street, and for good art galleries, look to Sutter Street between Kearny and Jones or the Civic Center area.

This page right A close view of the beautiful City Hall. Completed in 1915, it was the first of the many fine buildings making up the city's Civic Center.

Facing page Sausalito offers many speciality shops and restaurants on the waterside main street. Art galleries and antique shops abound, and writers and artists are now as numerous as the many yachtsmen.

Left Home for San Francisco's fishing fleet is here at Fisherman's Wharf, but there's not much room these days for mending nets and fixing boats. Fishermen's Wharf is not only the center of a commercial fishing industry, but a major tourist attraction with a lot else going on besides.

Above Alameda is an island city in San Francisco Bay. It used to be an aviation center, but today it is a naval air station, and container port.

Below left Look across the bay to San Francisco's beautiful skyline. It's a picture that keeps changing, but the pyramid-shaped Trans America building, rising to its spectacular pinnacle, is unlikely ever to be overshadowed.

Below right Fog suits chilly Alcatraz, for so long a federal penitentiary housing prisoners whom no other prison could contain. Al Capone was one of its more famous occupants. The island is 12 acres of uninviting rock surrounded by icy water with treacherous currents and the threat of sharks.

Above Several early Californian boats are moored at Hyde Street Pier, as part of the San Francisco Maritime Museum. The museum itself houses memorabilia of local maritime history. The museum and Pier are linked by the Aquatic Park, which has both gardens and a beach.

Left The strong winds and tides in the narrow strait of the Golden Gate provided a tough testing ground for all yachtsmen. The opening day of the yachting season is seen here from Golden Gate Bridge.

Right Cross Golden Gate Bridge or go by ferry to one of Marin County's most picturesque spots, Sausalito. Once a fishing village, it still has a Mediterranean atmosphere, and its views across the bay are superb. Sausalito is now San Francisco's yachting center with as many as 2 000 boats in its marinas.

Previous page At four and a half miles long the San Francisco-Oakland Bay Bridge is one of the world's longest. It was opened in 1936 at a cost of $77 200 000 and, although lacking the romantic delicacy of Golden Gate Bridge, it is still a remarkable sight.

69

Major Attractions

1 Union Square Downtown, and in the middle of the city's finest shops, Union Square is the place to take a break or meet your friends.

2 Fisherman's Wharf One of the liveliest spots in San Francisco; it's the center of the fishing industry, a shopping area, the haunt of the city's best street performers and the starting point for tours of Alcatraz.

3 Nob Hill Once home for the railroad barons, still home for the rich. Most of the splendid Victorian mansions were wiped out in the 1906 earthquake, and the only one to survive now houses the exclusive Pacific-Union Club.

Grace Cathedral at the top of Nob Hill, on the site of the former home of Charles Crocker, Grace Cathedral boasts bronze doors which are copies of the famous East doors of the Baptistry in Florence.

4 Coit Tower on Telegraph Hill. Built as a monument to the city's volunteer firemen, Coit Tower rises 210 feet from the summit of Telegraph Hill and gives superb views over the city.

5 Lombard Street 'The crookedest street in the world'. One block with eight switchback bends and abundant flower beds in between.

6 Golden Gate Park One thousand acres of lushious parkland developed from a wasteland. Golden Gate Park also contains three museums, an elaborate conservatory and a Japanese Tea Garden.

7 Palace of Fine Arts Originally a temporary structure built for the Panama-Pacific Exposition of 1915, it was later rebuilt in concrete. Inside children can learn about the mysteries of science from a vast array of gadgets.

8 Mission Dolores San Francisco was just a mission town that grew into a city. Mission Dolores is where the Franciscan Friars established their mission to convert the natives.

9 Fort Point Underneath Golden Gate Bridge, on the site of the 18th century Presidio, Fort Point was built in 1861 as part of the defense of the coastline.

10 California Palace of the Legion of Honor Situated in the middle of Lincoln Park golf course and housing a fine collection of French Art, this is a memorial for the American Soldiers killed in World War 1.

11 Chinatown Home to the largest group of Asians outside the Orient, Chinatown is a city within a city. The main thoroughfare, Grant Avenue, offers a choice of hundreds of restaurants and shops.

12 Broadway In the North Beach area, this is the street for entertainment. Sex shows of all kinds are on offer here. There are some good nightclubs too.

13 City Hall At the end of Fulton Street, the most impressive of the civic center buildings. It is modeled on the Capitol in Washington DC.

Wells Fargo History Room Headquarters of the Wells Fargo Company. Here you can rediscover Old California and the History of the Gold Rush.

14 Presidio This is where the Spanish built their garrison when they first came to settle in 1776. The Presidio now houses the United States Sixth Army.

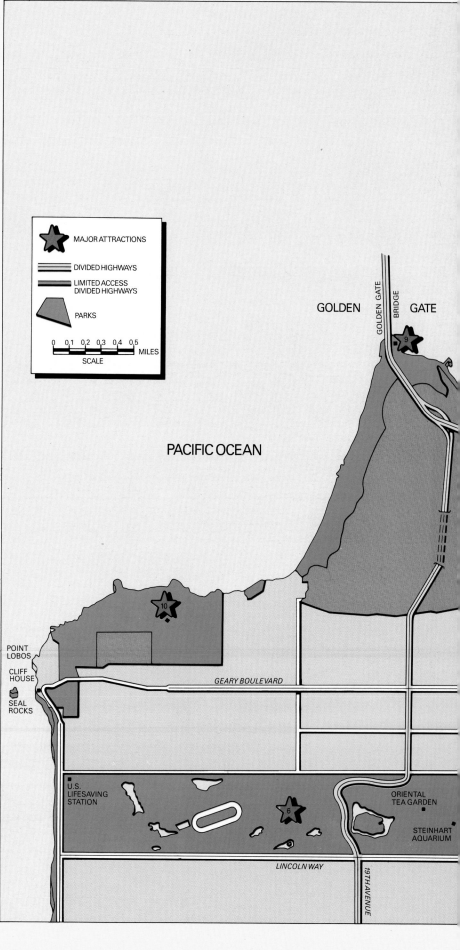

15 San Francisco Maritime Museum The museum of San Francisco's seafaring past. Photographs and relics trace the development of shipping from the Gold Rush to the present.

16 Balclutha A British trading ship first launched in 1886. The *Balclutha* has been restored by the San Francisco Maritime Museum and is open to the public.

Alcatraz Until 1963 a federal penitentiary containing infamous criminals such as Al Capone. The island has been open to the public since 1973, and tours leave daily from Fisherman's Wharf. (Not shown)

Sausalito A Mediterranean-style village across the Bay, in opulent Marin County. Sausalito is favored by yachtsmen, writers and artists. (Not shown)

Cable cars Invented in 1873 to help the San Franciscans get around their hilly city, cable cars are loved by tourists and strongly defended by the locals, despite their massive unprofitability. (Not shown)

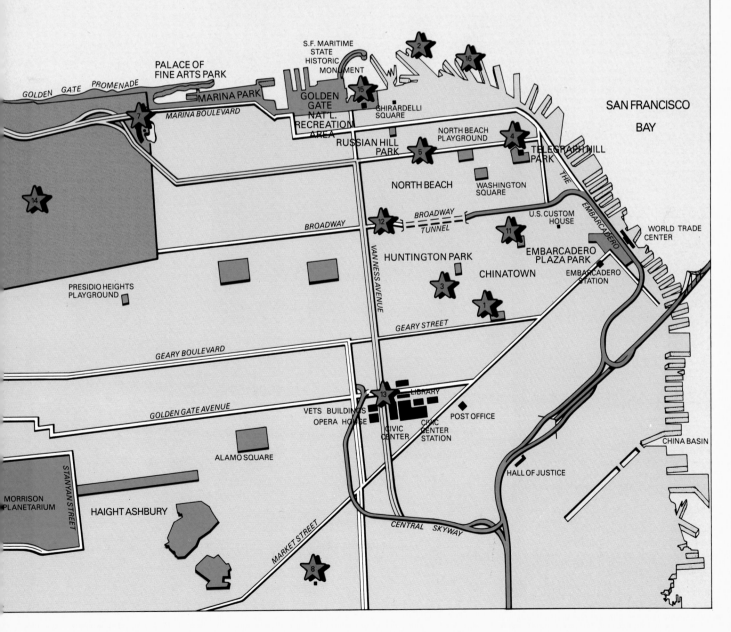

SAN FRANCISCO BAY

PALACE OF FINE ARTS PARK

S.F. MARITIME STATE HISTORIC MONUMENT

SAN FRANCISCO BAY

GOLDEN GATE PROMENADE

MARINA PARK

MARINA BOULEVARD

GOLDEN GATE NAT'L. RECREATION AREA

GHIRARDELLI SQUARE

RUSSIAN HILL PARK

NORTH BEACH PLAYGROUND

TELEGRAPH HILL PARK

NORTH BEACH

WASHINGTON SQUARE

BROADWAY

BROADWAY TUNNEL

U.S. CUSTOM HOUSE

THE EMBARCADERO

WORLD TRADE CENTER

HUNTINGTON PARK

EMBARCADERO PLAZA PARK

CHINATOWN

EMBARCADERO STATION

PRESIDIO HEIGHTS PLAYGROUND

VAN NESS AVENUE

GEARY STREET

GEARY BOULEVARD

LIBRARY

VETS BUILDINGS OPERA HOUSE

CIVIC CENTER

CIVIC CENTER STATION

POST OFFICE

GOLDEN GATE AVENUE

CHINA BASIN

ALAMO SQUARE

HALL OF JUSTICE

MORRISON PLANETARIUM

STANYAN STREET

HAIGHT ASHBURY

MARKET STREET

CENTRAL SKYWAY

PICTURE CREDITS

Camerapix Hutchison 11, 19 bottom, 21 bottom, 25 top, 26 top, 30 left and top right, 36 top, 38, 46, 64-65, 69   **Bruce Coleman Limited** 9 top, 10 top, 27 top, 33 top left and right, 36 bottom, 39 top, 45 top right and bottom, 52-53, 62-63, 64, 68   **Colourific!** 21 top and center, 22 bottom, 23 top, 47 right, 48 bottom, 51 bottom, 55 center, 58 top   **Daily Telegraph Colour Library** 14, 19 top, 20 bottom, 26 bottom, 31, 32, 49 bottom, 51 top, 60   **Brian Hawkes** 57 bottom   **Angelo Hornak** 35   **Ethel Hurwicz** 47 left   **The Image Bank** end papers, 1, 10 bottom, 15 top, 24, 30 bottom right, 37 top, 45 top left   **Kos** 57 top   **The Photo Source** 28-29, 41 bottom, 48 top, 72   **The Photographers' Library** 40 bottom, 44, 50, 54   **Rex Features** 39 bottom   **Frank Spooner Pictures** 15 bottom, 25 bottom, 34 bottom   **Tony Stone Associates** 8, 42-43, 56 bottom   **Vautier-de Nanxe** 22 top, 23 bottom, 27 bottom, 61   **Vision International** 12-13, 16-17, 20 top, 34 top, 37 bottom, 40 top, 41 top, 49 top, 65   **ZEFA** front cover, 2-3, 4-5, 6-7, 18, 55 top and bottom, 56 top, 58 bottom, 59, 68-69, back cover.

Multimedia Publications (UK) Limited have endeavored to observe the legal requirements with regard to the rights of suppliers of photographic material.